COLORS

AROUND ME

COLORS
AROUND ME

Vivian Church

***Illustrated by* Sherman Beck**

Copyright © 1971 by Afro-Am Publishing Company, Inc.
A Division of African American Images

Second revised printing

Printed through Colorcraft Ltd, Hong Kong
Printed in China

Library of Congress Catalog Card Number: 75-154209

Standard Book Number: 910030-15-4

COMMENTS FROM THE AUTHOR

Colors Around Me, a readiness book for the kindergarten and first-grade child, utilizes color in a new context. It is designed to develop a satisfying self-image through association with racial group identification. It focuses on color and race in order to develop reading as a personal meaningful experience. The technique was utilized because of its success with five and six-year-old children at the Abraham Lincoln Center on the South Side of Chicago.

The analogies of color, often suggested by the children, are associated with concrete symbols that are not only pleasant to the child, but universally pleasant. The child will begin, in such a setting, to identify positively with his color.

Colors Around Me further explains the meaning of the words "Black", "Negro", and "African American." Keener understanding of these widely, and sometimes loosely, used terms dispels confusion in the minds of young children.

Colors Around Me finally promotes race acceptance and unity. There is no better way for a child to begin reading than by studying himself, his friends, and his own culture. Because this book tells children about themselves and their culture, implications for the Black and White child are advantageous; for the former it is inspirational, for both it is educational.

Vivian E. Church

A WORD FROM THE PUBLISHER

African American Images/Afro-Am is committed to providing much needed materials such as these that will enable children to better understand the complex issues of race and color.

On the kindergarten-first grade level, *Colors Around Me* can be read to the pupil and the pictures shown and discussed. Words like beige, cinnamon, licorice, ebony, cooper and strong (as applied to coffee) can be clarified with meaningful pupil participation. The pictures and words are large to facilitate this type of teacher-pupil enjoyment of the book.

The second and third grade child should find the book interesting in spite of its simple text because of the concepts introduced. This book should be included in every second and third grade library along with related books to satisfy the resultant stimulation for further reading.

In this regard, African American Images/Afro-Am Publishing Company has produced a teacher's guide and a portfolio of study prints as companion materials to this book.

The portfolio of study prints, *Colors Around Us*, uses twelve of the illustrations from this book to expand the awareness of young children from the beauty of different skin colors to the wider awareness of different peoples in our nation and the world. With teacher assistance, these prints can be used as early as the first grade. Second and third grades may have to resort to the dictionary, but the information is presented in such an interesting way that the pupil will be eager to become involved in this activity.

African American people are

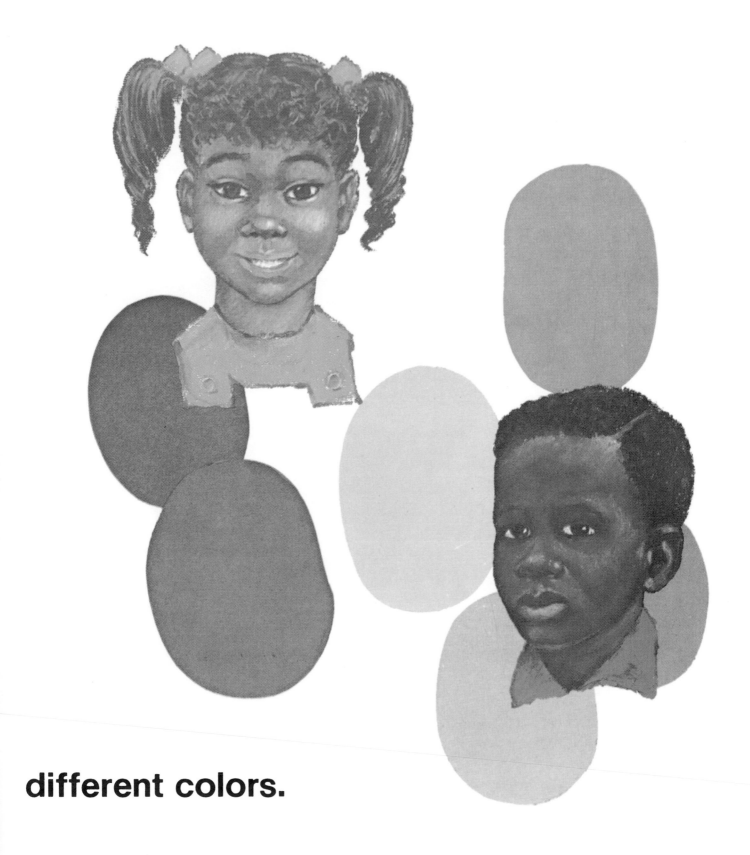

different colors.

Emily is brown like chocolate cake.

Robby is red like cinnamon rolls.

Sandra is beige like baked cookies.

Michael is black like licorice candy.

Victor is pink like bubble gum.

Sharon is tan like peanut butter.

Renee is golden like a peach.

12

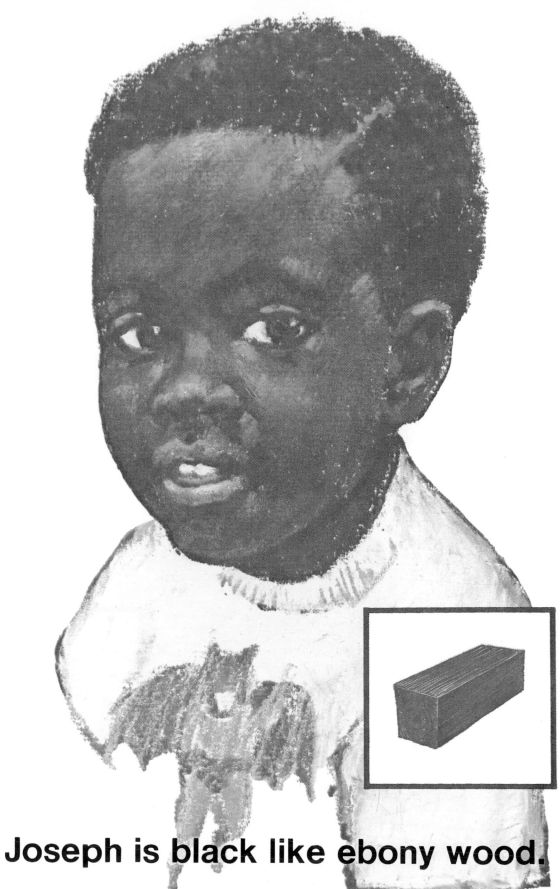

Joseph is black like ebony wood.

Debbie is black like strong coffee.

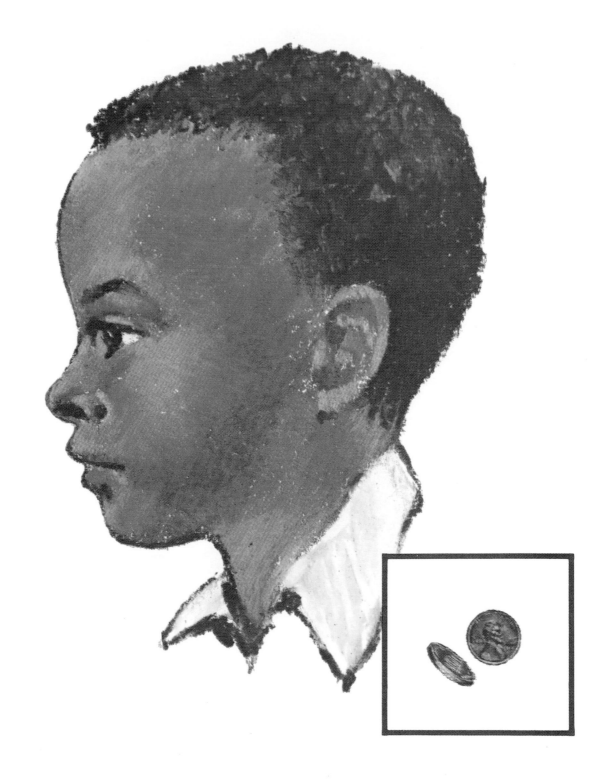

Stewart is brown like a copper penny.

Edward is brown like roast turkey.

Elesa is white like vanilla ice cream.

Kenny is yellow like a ripe pear.

Who are we?

What are we called?

And why?

JUST LIKE YOU.

JUST LIKE ME.